THE
PLEASURES
OF
FLY
FISHING

THE PLEASURES OF FLY FISHING

by V. S. HIDY

Photographs & Commentary on
Streams, Rivers, Lakes, Anglers, Trout & Steelhead.
Including a Selection of Memorable Observations from
the Classsic Writings of Angling Literature

WINCHESTER PRESS • NEW YORK • 1972

All rights reserved under International
and Pan American Copyright Conventions.

Library of Congress Catalog Card Number: 77-159428

ISBN: 0-87691-039-8

Designed by Visuality

Published by Winchester Press
460 Park Avenue, New York 10022

PRINTED IN JAPAN BY TOPPAN PRINTING COMPANY

Foreword

by Sparse Grey Hackle

Fish are, of course, indispensable to the angler. They give him an excuse for fishing and justify the flyrod without which he would be a mere vagrant. But the average fisherman's average catch doesn't even begin to justify, *as fish*, its cost in work, time, and money. The true worth of fishing, as the experienced, sophisticated angler comes to realize, lies in the memorable contacts with people and other living creatures, scenes and places, and living waters great and small which it provides.

Memorable, that is the key word. It is the recollection, the memory of all that the angler has experienced or observed, that changes the catching of a few fish for the frying pan into a yearlong and lifelong recreation. And it is these memories of days astream that lead the angler to find in the literature of the art those records and comments, that philosophizing of other anglers that he will delight to compare with his own.

In the field of memory the camera is, of course, the supreme tool. That little instrument, scarcely larger than two packs of cigarettes, is a remembering machine more potent and accomplished, for the angler's purposes, than the most highly developed computer with its "memory banks." It doesn't lie, that little machine, and it doesn't forget. For all your future days it brings back, strong and clear, the memories that have faded and become distorted in your mind; it sharpens again the worn and rounded edges of your recollections.

But I must remind you that it does these wonders only if you use it. I cannot recall anyone who was ever sorry that he took a picture, but I have heard, and myself have voiced, an infinite number of lamentations that some picture had not been taken.

The world would not know, ever, what George Edward Mackenzie Skues, the greatest fishing writer of his time and the creator of nymph fishing, looked like had not his friend Dr. E. A. Barton taken a wonderful, informal portrait of him with his injured wrists and his big hands that were so deft, his rod and his long-handled net and old, safety-pinned linen fishing bag, and the kindness and generosity he tried to hide behind a crusty expression.

If my dear friend, the late Dick Clark, had not handed his camera to a bystander to snap a picture of him and another old friend, Charlie Fox, sitting with me on the famous bench beside the placid Letort, I would not now have a picture to cherish as long as I live.

And if Bob Cunningham, a true artist with the lens, had not taken photographs of dreamlike beauty along the DeBruce Fly Fishing Club Water on the upper Willowemoc, his fellow-members would be beginning to forget even now how the Clubhouse Pond, the Junction Pool where George LaBranche cast his first dry fly, the Rhododendron Run, the Campsite Pool, and many another fair prospect looked before the catastrophic flood a couple of years ago.

In the following pages "Pete" Hidy shows, in text and picture, how a good fisherman, a good photographer, and a good student of the literature has collected and stored his memories.

Go thou and do likewise.

Preface

The curious madness of fly fishing attracts thousands of new devotees each year, sportsmen of all ages, who wish to deceive trout with a fly rather than mere bait. As novices they seek first to demonstrate their skills by catching the most fish. Next they want to catch the largest fish. Then, in the final and most delightful stage, they find the greatest pleasure in deceiving the more difficult or "problem" fish . . . and returning them to the water.

Releasing trout is evidence of a fly fisherman's maturity. He no longer needs to kill in order to enjoy his sport The words of Vance Bourjaily, novelist and teacher who fishes and hunts, express   it well: *"I assert that a man does not go fishing or hunting in order to obtain, or kill, as much game as he can. I assert that he does it in order to achieve a certain relationship between himself and wildness, to match himself against the land and against certain of its creatures, possession of which he has taught himself to desire. It is not merely his skill with rod and gun which he wants to exercise . . . there is a more spacious feeling, the feeling of free agency within a large solitude . . . the feeling of being alone and unhampered in one's pursuit, to follow it as one sees fit, by no man's sufferance."*

And so it is most especially with fly fishing. Despite the equipment mystique with which we all burden ourselves from time to time, the sport brings us closer to fundamental natural truths than our normal everyday pursuits. Asgeir Asgeirson, the former President of Iceland and a keen angler all his life, said it better than I: *"It is of no great matter how well a man fishes for there are so many other things. There is the countryside, the peace, the soothing murmur of the water in the river. All this has such a good effect on a person, especially if he is a tired city-dweller. You are in contact with Nature and things that have been part of man since time immemorial. Despite all the technical developments and space exploration and so forth, it would be perilous for man to lose contact with Nature. The link must never be broken.*

"Finally, there are one's good companions. To be in such peace with the bosom of Nature, I would say in some sort of communion with one's God, and together with trusted friends—there is nothing else that can provide such relaxation, tranquillity and reinvigoration."

The pleasures of fly fishing, of course, involve us with many things, many people and in many ways. Each angler seeks and finds his own pattern of involvement. This book is based on a dual pursuit that, over the years, has given me deep and lasting satisfaction—fly fishing and photography. The angler's camera, like his rod, becomes an intensely personal tool. Ultimately, his collections of slides and prints are as great a source of pleasure as his tackle and flies. Not for themselves as things, certainly, but for their power to evoke the magic of the days spent on the water.

The rationale for the angler-photographer has an appealingly simple logic. Exceptional picture-taking opportunities are abundant in the environments frequented by fly fishermen. We all fish in beautiful country. We want to capture those dramatic thunderheads in the sky along with the beauty of flowing water because there is an artist in many of us who readily senses the excitement of a picture situation.

In his book, *The Fish and the Fly*, John Atherton expresses the idea very well. *"When one thinks as an angler and an artist at the same time, not only angling but nature as a whole is involved. This integration has given new meaning to my contacts with the stream and its surroundings."*

Atherton, an accomplished professional artist as well as an amateur fly-tyer and photographer, goes on to confide that *"Angling is a contemplative recreation which brings the angler a particularly acute consciousness of his surroundings. He is frequently alone on the stream. His conversation, if it can be called that, is with nature rather than individuals. He is made subtly aware of nature's reaction to his presence there."*

For this fisherman, at least, photography adds an exciting dimension to any day on any water. In the words of Jacques-Henri Lartigue, *"Picture-taking is a trap of images—serious, fleeting, funny, tragic, fanciful, rare, human, irreplaceable."* For the angler, pictures are a record of our passing through a valuable and irreplaceable environment . . . the simple joys of appreciating the changing moods and beauty created by clouds, wind, sunlight, and shadows.

This relates comfortably and purposefully to the recent universal concern for ecology and the preservation of our various environments. In one of the beautiful publications of the Sierra Club, *Time and the River Flowing*, Aldo Leopold, Loren Eiseley, and Wallace Stegner are quoted to dramatize the importance of water and our relationship to water. Leopold was a devoted fly fisherman throughout his life.

Loren Eiseley: *"If there is magic on this planet, it is contained in water. Water reaches everywhere; it touches the past and prepares the future; it moves under the poles and wanders thinly in the heights of the air."*

Aldo Leopold: *"The good life on any river may depend on the perception of its music, and the preservation of some music to perceive."*

Wallace Stegner: *" . . . the deliberate refusal to make any marks at all . . . to leave the beauty spots scrupulously alone—because our species needs sanctuaries."*

The fly fisherman with a camera in his creel leaves his sanctuaries scrupulously unmarked . . . carrying on his contemplative conversation with nature . . . achieving

a certain relationship between himself and wildness...within a large solitude...
perceiving the music of the river. When he kills a fish or two for the fire, he does
so in the spirit of "harvesting the crop." With his camera, however, he harvests
an inexhaustible, perpetually renewable resource of pleasure. In the words of
Edward Steichen, *"There is an excitement about using the camera that never
gets used up."*

This book is an outward and visible sign of my inward and spiritual involvement with Nature, fishing, and photography. It started out as pretty much a
picture album. Then, as a longtime admirer of classic angling literature I thought
of the great pleasure fly fishermen receive from reading the half-forgotten
masterpieces of earlier angling writers. The imagery of words together with the
photographs would accomplish my goal of portraying some of the mystery of
fly fishing to those who ask "What is this fly fishing all about?" Here is the
beauty of natural amphitheaters we go back to time and again; here is the
magic of trout streams . . . a love of the contest with discriminating fish in all
kinds of weather . . . the exuberant but careful strategy of capturing trout with
delicate tackle and fragile feather flies in a manner which both of the
participants can enjoy and appreciate.

V. S. Hidy

Robinson Bar Ranch
Sunbeam, Idaho
10 August 1970

ACKNOWLEDGMENTS

For arrangements made with various authors, their representatives and publishers, where copyrighted material was permitted to be reprinted, and for the courtesy extended by them, the following acknowledgments are gratefully made:

Adam & Charles Black, Ltd. for selections from *Golden Days* by Romilly Fedden, copyright 1949 by A. & C. Black; for selections from *Halcyon* by George Brennand, copyright 1947 by A. & C. Black.

William Morrow & Company, Inc. for selections from *A River Never Sleeps* by Roderick Haig-Brown, copyright 1946 by Roderick Haig-Brown; for selections from *Fisherman's Fall* by Roderick Haig-Brown, copyright 1964 by Roderick Haig-Brown.

Geoffrey Bles Ltd. for selections from *River Keeper* by John Waller Hills, copyright 1947 by Geoffrey Bles.

Putnam & Co. Ltd. for selections from *My Rod My Comfort* by Sir Robert Bruce Lockhart, copyright 1949 by Putnam & Co.

Harvey and Blythe Ltd. for selections from *Within The Streams* by John Hillaby, copyright 1949 by John Hillaby.

William Heinemann Ltd. for selections from *Trout from the Hills* by Ian Niall, copyright 1961 by Ian Niall; for selections from *The New Poacher's Handbook* by Ian Niall, copyright 1960 by Ian Niall.

Chatto & Windus for selections from *Alexander and Angling* by R. Sinclair Carr, copyright 1936 by R. Sinclair Carr.

Dodd, Mead & Co. for selections from *No Life So Happy* by Edwin L. Peterson, copyright 1940 by Dodd, Mead & Co., publishers.

Touchstone Press for selections from *A Leaf From French Eddy* by Ben Hur Lampman, copyright 1966 by Lena Lampman.

Howard T. Walden, 2d. for selections from *Upstream and Down* by Howard T. Walden, 2d.

Richard Ciccimarra for selections from *The Cowichan* published in *The Creel* by The Flyfisher's Club of Oregon.

J. M. Dent & Sons, Ltd. for selections from *Fly Fishing* by Viscount Grey of Fallodon.

Little, Brown & Co. for selections from *Pools and Ripples* by Bliss Perry, copyright 1927 by Bliss Perry.

THE
PLEASURES
OF
FLY
FISHING

Where Would You Go?

Where would you go? With the will and way of it, and never a
care for time, nor a fret for absence, and all of an eagerness,
where would you go?...

He said that he would go to a purple canyon, south and south of here, where of mornings the shadows are long and magical, and when you come to the creek for water the deer have been there but a moment before. And all the voices of the canyon are of the trees, and the creek, and the whistling flutter of a wild drake's wing low above the brisk current. And all the odors of the canyon are of leaf and fern and a wetness of rocks that are liveried in moss, and the good odor of fallen trees that yield themselves to earth both graciously and gratefully. And because of this, all this, there is a certain peacefulness and healing in the purple canyon not elsewhere to be encountered . . . .

When it is noon in the purple canyon and the sun soars slowly
over the forest and hills as a golden hawk, the rounded boulders
of the creek shimmer and dance in the warmth of the sun,
and on the countenance of the cliff, where every crevice has
its flower in blossom, the warmth of the ancient sun is pooled
for a blue lizard drowsing. There is a silence of sunshine then
in the canyon, and silver and silent the trout are drowsing
under the emerald and spume. How far away, and yet how
near and clement, is the blue curvature of heaven.

Where Would You Go?
Ben Hur Lampman

Opening Day

Where shall we go, you say? Let's go back to the place where the tall fern is parted under the firs at the brink of the canyon, and the black trail plunges down, with handholds of sapling and root, to white water — down, down to the South Fork. With the salmonberry blooming, and the blue grouse hooting, and somewhere a wild pigeon mourning its heart out. The voice of the South Fork comes up from the canyon till the air pulses with it, and as you go down, down, where the deer have gone, you glimpse the tossed swiftness of the long rapids. Now the last few yards of the trail are steep as a church roof — but here, gray-walled and clamoring, unforgotten, with a hatch dancing above the green swirl by the black rock, here is the South Fork. Do you remember? Let's go back....

Do you remember? Yonder's the log jam that was many a freshet in making, and the green water lifts without foam as the river slips under the barrier. If trout come out from under the satiny weave of it, they are likely to be large fish, and from much dwelling in shadow are apt to be darkly gleaming. And they will strike where the water lifts — instant and visible and strong. It is a place where the water ouzel sings, as once we heard him; a place where the swifts hunt the little wind of the canyon, for the fly hatch, as once we saw them. It is a place where the mink stares at you, wonderingly, glistening. How far, how very far above, the canyon's brink seems. How small the firs and how fore-shortened. The hawk calls as he crosses over. And wild, and fond, and far the place is, and beyond the log jam is the great bar and the long riffle. Let's go back....

Where shall we go, you say? Let's go back to the place where the paunchy, lithe, shining grandfather of all trout rose thrice, and at the third rise struck smashingly — to leap unbelievably! The reel sings. Not under the trailing branch! Not there! Back to the place where you beached the big trout, bigger even than he had seemed, and the sunshine that fell on the sandbar warmed the rose of his flanks and his cheeks, and the green, and the gold, and the silver and all the glory of him. And plain on the sand is the print of the cougar's great paw. So that one looks at the tangled steepness, up and up to the brink of the cayon — looks and wonders. And here a trout and there a trout, and each of us wet to the armpits, and a sort of feeling that we have come home again. Let's go back.

Do you remember? Well, then, let's go back to the canyon of the South Fork — or someplace — where we used to go. To get so tired from the fishing, but never of fishing, that the very ache of our tiredness is good to feel. Back where we used to go. Let's skirt the black cliff again hazardously — watch out for that rodtip! — and fish once more to the bend and then take time off to make coffee over a driftwood fire. And lie on the sand with a tussock of clover for pillow and from under the brims of our hats watch the high clouds wander over. And lie on the sand and talk, or keep silent, and wonder about how far the car is. And count our trout, maybe, and clean them. It is odd about happiness. The hour glass that measures it is both swift and slow. Do you remember the place where we used to fish? Let's go back.

A Leaf From French Eddy
Ben Hur Lampman

It is the spirit of fishing, its immeasurable charm and mystery, which ever leads us on beyond the woods where the wild birds sing. Never can we reach our final goal, for always before us lie further fields yet to explore.

Golden Days
Romilly Fedden

An Infinity of Variables

I am afraid most of us who are ordinary run-of-the-mill fishermen, fishing rather varied waters under varying conditions, have to count on having our theories upset from time to time, and I doubt if we should complain about it or resent it. Undoubtedly fish have patterns of behavior that are roughly predictable and we can afford to take pride in our understanding of these patterns and the successes that grow from it....

... But fortunately we are working always with an infinity of variables that would drive any scientist to distraction — season, temperature, current, light, the aberrations of the fish themselves, their senses and perceptions and perhaps even the aberrations of insects. We may be able to tidy all this into a nice workable theory from time to time and gain greatly from it, but I do not think we need feel ashamed or rejected when such a theory falls apart. It is better to summon back a youthful contempt for experience and some of youth's keenness and boldness in experiment.

Fisherman's Fall
Roderick Haig-Brown

The Stuff of Dreams

If I had a choice of skills and could go back in life to make the choice and use the skill, I should ask simply for the angler's skill and no more. Let everything else be as it is in reality; let fishing be no easier, let me catch nothing a great deal better than the trout I have caught, but let me have time ahead to fish and with that I should have the stuff of dreams, and be content.

Trout from the Hills
Ian Niall

Second Sight

The man who isn't aware of atmosphere lacks the
making of a good trout fisherman — I am sure of that.
I believe in second sight... nearly always my
successes have come as a result of a feeling that
I was about to catch a fish in a certain bit of water
and this invariably when I had a feeling for the
place, sensing its moods and, perhaps, the reaction
of the fish.

Trout from the Hills
Ian Niall

Water

"Of all inorganic substances, acting in their own proper nature, and without assistance or combination, water is the most wonderful. If we think of it as the source of all the changefulness and beauty which we have seen in clouds...

...then as the instrument by which the earth we have contemplated was modelled into symmetry, and its crags chiselled into grace...

. . .then as, in the form of snow, it robes the
mountains it has made, with that transcendent light
which we could not have conceived if we had not
seen; then as it exists as the form of the torrent —
in the iris which spans it, in the morning mist
which rises from it, in the deep crystalline pools
which mirror its hanging shore, in the broad lake
and glancing river; finally, in that which is to all
human minds the best emblem of unwearied,
unconquerable power, the wild, various, fantastic,
tameless unity of the sea. . .

...what shall we compare to this mighty, this universal element, for glory and for beauty? Or how shall we follow its eternal changefulness of feeling?

"Of Truth of Water,"
Modern Painting
John Ruskin

Constant Imagination

Persevere with a constant imagination to obtain
pleasure and satisfaction. The angler must entice,
not command, his reward...

    That which is worth millions to his contentment
another may buy for a groate in the market.

The Pleasures of Princes
Gervase Markham

The True Joy of Angling

The true joy of angling does not lie in the number of trout caught; it does not lie in a knowledge of the history of the art, nor a wide knowledge of flies, nor in the ability to astound uninitiated listeners with a display of piscatorial profundity.

It lies in something more human and more real than any of these — in the perception of the poetry of a day on a mountain stream, a day that begins with the warble of an operatic robin and ends with the Keatsian contralto of the whippoorwill. In between are a host of impressions, connotations, reflections, realizations, aspirations, that leave not a dull moment from the first purple of dawn to the afterglow of sunset. And we have that most poetic of all the lesser arts, the laying of the fly. None unacquainted with fly casting can quite understand the satisfaction and the joy of creation which come with the skillful performance of this part of angling.

We are standing, let us say, on a submerged rock near the middle of a stream. There is the tug of water about our knees and hips, the feel of water moss beneath our feet, the rush of rapids in our ears, the brown foam and the green of hemlock and willow, side by side, before our eyes. Far upstream — far measured by a fly caster's sense of distance — lies a square yard of water, gently swirling, blackly deep. In that mysterious swirl lies, we know, or think we know, a brook trout, one of splendid coloring and dark courage. We select from our box of flies a Quill Gordon, olive and blue, conservative, almost as light as the air through which it falls. With a General Turle knot, we attach the fly invisibly at the end of a four-x leader, thin as cobweb. . . .

The fairy three-and-one-half-ounce rod whips the Quill Gordon dryly through the air. She must travel forty feet through hemlock scent without touching a twig before or behind. She must curve gently to the right of a hemlock bough overhanging a splotch of yellow foam, yet must fall six inches short of a green-brown log at the head of the little square of water. She must light gently, like the breast feather of a song sparrow, before either the leader or the line. Immediately, the leader must sink into invisbility. The Quill Gordon must float, titillate, imperiously, for a fleet five seconds on the surface of the swirling black, before the leader, caught in the swift current below, begins to drag the fly with an obvious wake. And in that five seconds of perfect fly floating, the trout must see, must desire, and must rise.

For a moment, we seem to be part of the water and of the hemlock-scented air. We make preliminary casts, lengthen them, draw a deep breath, try to keep muscles relaxed, flick the fly out with the fairy wand, direct the rod tensely to the right, release line quickly as the leader begins to straighten, see the leader curve to the right, whisping past the hemlock bough like an abstract pattern, and see the Quill Gordon drop as lightly as a cat's foot on the churning water. From the depths comes a golden flash, a rainbow spray, a sudden pumping of the rod, and the contest is on....

The line curves through foam and rapid, the rod bends like
something living, the sun flashes on a variegated arc, then on
another, the tip lowers, the rod vibrates, comes straight, bends
again, and at last the trout is at the angler's feet, shaking his
head in wonderment at the eccentricities of flies. A net slides
gently under him, and he sparkles up into the hemlock-scented
air. In the willow creel he comes to rest, the willow creel lined
with ferns and wild flowers if the angler is a poet and the trout
a prince; in the foaming water is his release if the angler is a
sentimentalist and the trout a king. Then the hook is but a
pinprick and a memory, but the duel is a thing of beauty, a
poetry of motion, color and sound. It is like the improvisation
of music, and there is nothing left at the end but the
joy of creation....

Nothing left but the recollection of beauty, the shadow of a
laurel blossom on a pool, the shimmer of sunlight on riffles,
the recollection of our first trout, the awareness of the wetness
of drops of water, the companionship of rock, shadow, and
cloud, and the hope that somewhere, sometime, moments
such as these grow to eternity.

No Life So Happy
Edwin L. Peterson

Wild and Remote

He preferred trout streams that were wild and remote. You
couldn't please him with simple fishing, indolent, tame and
effortless fishing, though you promised a full creel.
He wanted the tangled slope of a mountain, a dim trail, a
contest with undergrowth and cliff, on the way to his stream....

And nobody there, when at length he broke through the brush
and gained the white water, save a friend and himself — and
a water wren teetering on a wet rock. A rainbow or a cutthroat
won from such a stream had thrice the value of greater fish
taken elsewhere without toil and within sound of traffic.

"A Farewell to 'Tige'"
Ben Hur Lampman

Philosophical Detachment

He is watching it, not with the sentimentalist's pre-occupation with pure beauty, but rather with the fisherman's trained perception of the effect of wind and light, of deeper or darker colored water, of eddy or shallow upon the next cast of his fly.

He must, of course, to perceive it fully, have a certain capacity for philosophical detachment, a kind of Oriental superiority to failure or success. Perhaps that is what being a "born fisherman" means.

Pools and Ripples
Bliss Perry

Something Delightfully Unpredictable

There is a mystery about the river, as keenly felt
today as it must have been felt many centuries ago,
of a different world in a different element. The
dividing line is the surface of the water, and there is
something delightfully unpredictable in our very
slight ability to penetrate the mystery....

... Absolute success is luckily impossible; and our most fervent hope must always be that even today's scientific progress will always leave some of the mystery unfathomed. However, we must also be grateful to progress — for, by affecting so much around us, it has renewed in us an awareness of old values which, a short time ago, we might have taken for granted.

"The Cowichan"
Richard Ciccimara

I confess that I have derived more pleasure from the environment of my fishing ventures than from the capture of fish. However good the sport may be, I have never cared for angling in the public gaze. My preference is for the lonely mountain stream whose course, from the small trickle on the hillside to the river mouth, is like the course of man's own journey through life.

My Rod My Comfort
Sir Robert Bruce Lockhart

A Primitive Curiosity

In the last analysis, though, it must be the fish
themselves that make fishing — the strangeness and
beauty of fish, their often visible remoteness, their
ease in another world, the mystery of their
movements and habits and whims. The steelhead
lying in the summer pool, the brown trout rising
under the cut bank, the Atlantic salmon rolling over
his lie, the bass breaking in the lily pads, the grayling
glimpsed in the rapid, the enormous unseen trout
cruising the lake's drop-off, all these are irresistible
temptations to anyone who has held a rod.

It is not that one wants to kill, though kill one may.
The appeal is more nearly that of hidden treasure,
except that this treasure has life and movement
and uncertainty beyond anything inanimate. The
thought in the mind is: "Let me try for him." The
desire is to stir the reaction, respond to it, control it;
to see the mystery close by in the water, perhaps
to handle it, to admire, to understand a little.
Perhaps it adds up to nothing more than a primitive
curiosity, but if so it remains powerful and lasting.

Fisherman's Fall
Roderick Haig-Brown

54

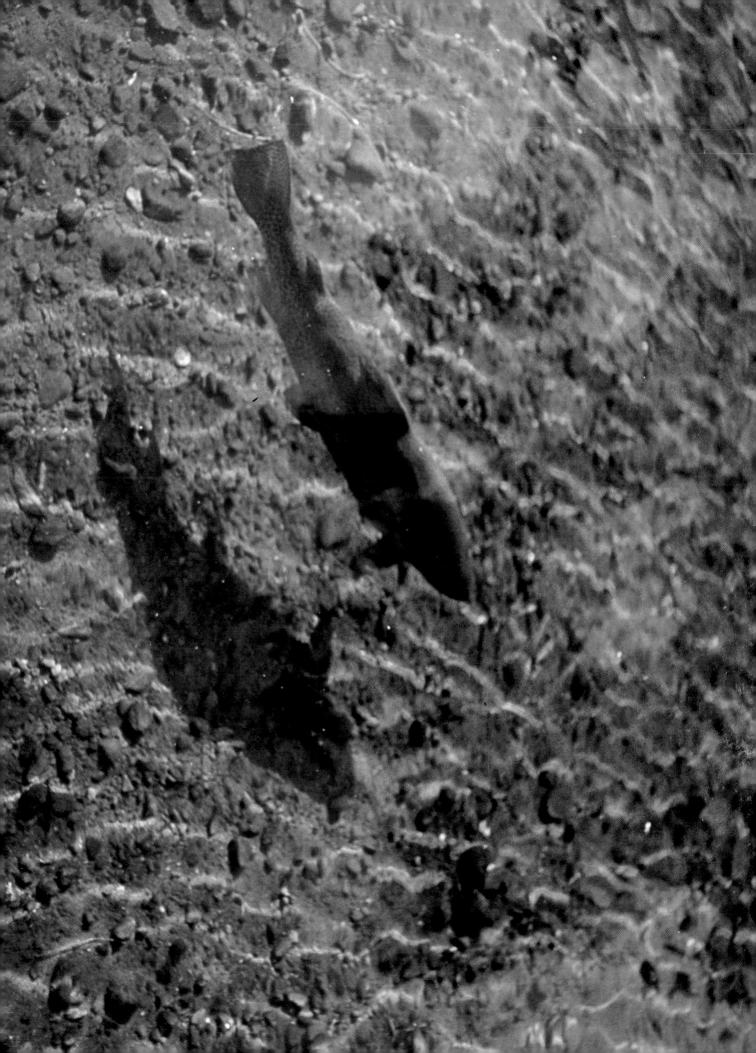

The Utter Beauty of the Trout

There is a detailed perfection about the trout that
even a fresh-run salmon cannot quite equal, and the
smell of a trout freshly caught; all the elusive
fragrance of weeds and moss and stones, washed
by rushing clean water, seems to cling about it.
The scent of water-falls, splashing through bracken
fronds and on the pale-green leaves of daffodils.
The trout seems to mirror the dappled shadows of
sunlight of eternally repeated summers, and the
glint of showery springtimes. The utter beauty of
the trout is one of the few illusions that to me has
remained undimmed for thirty-five years.

Halcyon
George Brennand

A Time for the Finer Points

I got into the water, walked along the firm ridge and made my
way along to the far bank. The dry sand-bed was surrounded
by a natural amphitheatre. In front of me there was the pool,
rippled now and again as a fish rolled over on to its side to
seize the little spinners that were coming down on the current
in lines. I scooped one of them out with my landing net. It was
a frail fly with glassy, iridescent wings, one of the Olives
species. To be quite sure I netted a few more as they floated
past with out-stretched wings, and gloried at being in such a
place at the time of such a definite hatch.

A Ginger Quill was the nearest imitation in the fly box.
Together in the palm of my hand there seemed to be no points
of resemblance between the two and my heart sank that
imitation could go no further. The live creature had filigree
wings. The body was pale amber, almost transparent, and the
tiny setae were threadlike, finer than anything I had in my box.
But I thanked heaven that my finest honey dun hackles
had gone into the Quill. Beside the real insect, the body
was coarse and opaque. Like so many of my flies it was far
too thick, but the wings had a glassy sparkle. Perhaps in a
flowing stream the fish would notice no difference....

It was a time for the finer points of fly fishing. I wrapped the line around my creel in loose folds and carefully greased it. I tied on a three-yards cast, tapered down to the finest gut in my case; I dipped the little Quill in paraffin and blew on it till it dried. For an emergency I dipped another one in readiness. They would have to float as no flies had floated before.

Everything was ready.

The first cast was really not my best effort. I made three false casts in the air, shot the line and put a long furl of gut in the bubbles of the waterfall. The line itself was in deeper water and the inevitable drag pulled the fly across the stream and against the flow of the water. It was very properly ignored.

I moved two feet into the river and cast again, almost straight upstream. The fly straightened out, bobbed on the surface once or twice—I was fearfully conscious of a projecting loop of gut near the eye of the hook—and then it popped under the water. It just disappeared. There was no visible rise. No floundering on the surface—just a fly that was there and then was there no longer....

I struck. The reel screamed a little and I felt the fish. It was another occasion for textbook tactics. I did everything in my power to keep it out of the pool where it would disturb the other fish, and the tackle took the strain manfully. Three yards away from me it decided to execute a corkscrew roll in the water. It turned over and over, gave a final kick, and then slid into my landing net — a grayling, just over the half pound.

As I took the fly out of its mouth another fish rose in the pool. It took the insect from the surface of the water with a movement that was like nothing so much as a kiss. There was a perfect economy of effort in the motion. No flounder or splash. Just a light intake of water and another fly had disappeared.

Within the Streams
John Hillaby

There Is Nothing Like the Fly

I don't know which is the most exciting; the thud
when a fish takes the wet fly under the water, the
'sip' as some big fish will turn and take a dry fly
down—just before you hit him—or the last moments
when you are, anxiously, about to land him. All of
them of course surpass anything that a spinning
bait can give you. There is nothing like the fly,
or the pleasure of casting it.

Going Fishing
Negley Farson

Exquisite Tools & Precise Manipulation

Fly fishing calls for the most precise and fastidious
manipulation of exquisitely fashioned tools.
A three-or four-ounce split-bamboo rod, with a
well-balanced reel, a tapered casting-line, a leader
of the proper fineness, and a well-tied fly, or flies,
is one of the most perfectly designed and executed
triumphs of human artisanship. A violin is
but little better....

At its pitch of dainty perfection it delights both the eye and the tactile sense, for not every rod which is beautifully made has the crowning virtue of the right "feel." And that it should look right and feel right as it comes to you from the skilled workman is only a part of the visual and manual pleasure which it yields.

For you, with your quite individual bodily and mental habits, your slowly acquired art as a fisherman, must now use this fragile combination of wood and steel and silk and gut and feathers under the most subtly variable conditions of light, wind and water.

Pools and Ripples
Bliss Perry

One Cast Above the Stone

I long since concluded that the best chance of raising
a good trout is the first time you cast over him,
providing that first is unheralded by either
movement or shadow. My best trout last year came
to me when I was secretly behind a boulder. The
stone fly was out and I was wading straight up the
middle of a shallow. I found myself behind a boulder
which almost entirely obscured me. Instead of
turning to the right or left, which was my proper
way, I thought 'Try one cast above that stone.' I did,
and a trout cut through the water to the fly
just like a shark.

Alexander and Angling
R. Sinclair Carr

A Golden Chance

But the river itself was the greatest fascination.
Its slow current hid things that I could only
vaguely imagine.
   I was almost genuinely afraid at times, afraid of
dragging the fly away from some crashing rise or of
jamming the reel as a great fish jumped or of doing
any of the hundred other things I could do to throw
away a golden chance.

A River Never Sleeps
Roderick Haig-Brown

Yellowstone

The Yellowstone River has occasion to run through a
gorge about eight miles long. To get to the bottom
of the gorge it makes two leaps, one of about one
hundred and twenty and the other of three hundred
feet. I investigated the upper or lesser fall, which
is close to the hotel.

Up to that time nothing particular happens to the
Yellowstone — its banks being only rocky, rather
steep, and plentifully adorned with pines.

At the falls it comes round a corner, green, solid,
ribbed with a little foam, and not more than thirty
yards wide. Then it goes over, still green, and rather
more solid than before. After a minute or two you,
sitting upon a rock directly above the drop, begin
to understand that something has occurred; that the
river has jumped between solid cliff walls, and that
the gentle froth of water lapping the sides of the
gorge below is really the outcome of great waves.

And the river yells aloud; but the cliffs do not
allow the yells to escape....

That inspection began with curiosity and finished in terror, for it seemed that the whole world was sliding in chrysolite from under my feet. I followed with the others round the corner to arrive at the brink of the canyon. We had to climb up a nearly perpendicular ascent to begin with, for the ground rises more than the river drops. Stately pine woods fringe either lip of the gorge, which is the gorge of the Yellowstone. You'll find all about it in the guide-books.

All that I can say is that without warning or preparation I looked into a gulf seventeen hundred feet deep with eagles and fish-hawks circling far below. And the sides of that gulf were one wild welter of color — crimson, emerald, cobalt, ochre, amber, honey splashed with port wine, snow white, vermilion, lemon, and silver gray in wide washes. The sides did not fall sheer, but were graven by time, and water, and air into monstrous heads of kings, dead chiefs — men and women of the old time. So far below that no sound of its strife could reach us, the Yellowstone River ran a finger-wide strip of jade green.

The sunlight took those wondrous walls and gave fresh hues to those that nature had already laid there.

Evening crept through the pines that shadowed us, but the full glory of the day flamed in that canyon as we went out very cautiously to a jutting piece of rock — blood-red or pink it was — that overhung the deepest deeps of all.

Now I know what it is to sit enthroned amid the clouds of sunset as the spirits sit in Blake's pictures. Giddiness took away all sensation of touch or form, but the sense of blinding color remained.

When I reached the main-land again I had sworn that I had been floating. Two of us crawled down to the Yellowstone — just above the first little fall — to wet a line for good luck. The round moon came up and turned the cliffs and pines into silver; and a two-pound trout came up also, and we slew him among the rocks, nearly tumbling into that wild river.

American Notes
Rudyard Kipling

A Little Below the Surface

These wild orgies...to see great fish walloping about like porpoises, too intent on their meal to take any notice of the fisherman, looking as though they could be caught by any duffer who could chuck a fly anyhow, to believe that you have before you many a splendid prize easy to be won, and then to come home with nothing, is an experience which knocks the conceit out of the most exalted.

I had a sharp lesson one August night from a friend, a great and ingenious angler, who was fishing with me at Stockbridge. Trout rose well: there was a noble hatch of blue-winged olive: I got nothing, he got two brace. He discovered, and I did not, that trout were taking the nymph a little below the surface.

River Keeper
John W. Hills

78

My Monster Was Free

Let me never fish again if a big trout should catch me without
a net! Being taken by a fish one simply cannot land is the
most mortifying experience an angler can have, whether
he is a philosopher or not.

I remember the afternoon this happened to me. I had been
weary long before noon and reduced to despair through my
line sinking so often that I was ready to give up before the
afternoon sun had begun to look over my shoulder, but I went
to fish in that corner where I had taken so many fine trout and
stood a while watching the odd fish rising far out in the little

bay. While I was doing this I saw a fish rise close in under the rocks. It was a good fish. The rise was characteristic of a big fish in that lake. I didn't wait but flicked the line on to the water with a backhand cast. The fly bounced against the rock face and dropped within two or three inches where, a second before, the fish had risen. Before I could balance my body the fish had taken the fly. I let line go, recovered my balance and began to play the fish. It was well hooked and ran first to the left and then to the right, keeping perhaps four or five inches below the surface but making no attempt to go down. It passed me quite close on the third or fourth occasion and I was astonished to see the sort of fish I was into. Here was a fish that some people might have called a cannibal. I began to guess as to its girth and weight. In any other water it could have been a salmon, I felt. Minutes passed and it came quite close to the side. I was able to look down on it and see the almost casual movement of fins, tail and mouth as it gaped.

It is a strange thing that many a well-hooked fish reserves its final strength for the moment when it is about to be captured. Let a fish run. Let it have line and tire it out in taking it. Bring it back under strain, but if it wants to, let it run again, let it run. There is no mystery in the business of playing a fish but one small fear assails me on these occasions. The hook, being a fly hook and not a treble, has time, through the fish moving first to the right and then to the left, through varying strain and the struggles of the fish to free himself, to work a hole and, unless it is burying itself deep in firm jaw, it may come out. One rarely learns why a fish gets away. Essentially it gets away because the hook comes out and the answer is to take no more time in handling a fish than is necessary to bring it, subdued, to the net or gaff....

This time I had no net or gaff. When the trout looked at me, hovering above the water with my rod curved as only a beautiful split cane rod can curve, it decided to be off again and this time it went down, straining the line over its back as it shook its head. A big trout shakes its head like a water spaniel, or a worrying dog, I always feel. It grows to be a big trout by learning how to live. In a minute my monster was free. I hardly saw him go. He moved into the deeps steadily and quite unlike a small trout when he has broken free. He didn't come back and he hasn't come back on any of the occasions I have waited for him in that place.

Trout from the Hills
Ian Niall

When a Big One Gets Away

Returning a good fish to the water will fill you with a sweet
and secret pride and leave no residuum of regret. There is an
awareness of material loss, perhaps, as there may be in the
donation of a handsome gift to charity, but the spiritual
gain outweighs it.

It is only when you lose a big one midway in the battle that
the shock of loss seems insupportable. The ensuing emotion is
comparable to nothing else in the whole psychological
experience of humans. There is a more profound and most
lasting sense of loss, but there is none more momentarily
acute than that which seizes you when a big one gets away.

For an interval that is not measurable in time your whole
being has been dedicated to that heavy throbbing resistance on
the end of your line. That pull of the fish against your wrist and
against all your hopes and prayers is perhaps the perfect
emotional satisfaction, the ultimate of evanescent Nirvana, the
complete if momentary solvent of all the mundane cares which
can beset a man. Its natural consummation, the capture, is the
good aftermath of ecstasy; but the thwarting of that end is
frustration in its most real and bitter form. He is a philospher
and a sportsman, indeed, who can smile as his pressure is
suddenly unrequited, that tautness suddenly slack.

Upstream and Down
Howard T. Walden, II

You Can Never Forget

You may forget the fish that you catch or lose, but you can never forget the fishing. No two successive hours are alike to the angler, for the brook or river is changing its form and hue in every instant, and his mind and mood and artistry are affected by every yard of the gliding stream.

Pools and Ripples
Bliss Perry

Familiar Streams and Strange Waters

There are many anglers who go to the same stream year after year. They do not even go to a different part of that stream. The same hotel sees them at the same time of the year, and they repeat the joys and sorrows of their previous visit with but little variation.

They begin by having the same breakfast in the same room. They expect the same pictures on the walls and would miss the faded places in the well-remembered wallpaper. They make the same remarks to the same waitress, and they would be full of bitterness were they not served with bacon and eggs on the same kind of plates, and tea from familiar cups.

They enjoy this seeing of the same things in the same place. They expect the stream to be just as it

was a year ago. If a tree has been uprooted in the winter of their absence they are sad. If a pool has changed in contour, having yielded to the turbulence of a freshet, they are filled with chagrin. They look with something near to irritation at a sandbank which has shifted queerly north to south in deference to the force of February waters.

As they depart to their customary starting place their remarks to all who may be there to listen are as of yore. When they return their catch varies but little from the old days. Most of their explanations of it have been listened to so often that even those who do not hear them remember without difficulty what reply to make.

There is a fascination in this visiting of familiar streams. You become familiar with them at considerable cost. You believe that all this care and trouble will be turned to better purpose each time you go. Each bend, each streamy shallow, each smoothly flowing deep, each shady corner, every overhanging bank and every cowering boulder, all these have their significance at each repeated visit. They seem to grow more important as they are oftener seen.

Are we more successful on these familiar streams? Does local knowledge reduce our handicap and add numbers to our catch? I would prefer you to answer these questions for yourselves for I am not too sure.

There is no gainsaying the curious charm of fishing familiar streams again and yet again. But there is no certainty that this recurring effort in the end means better baskets. Perhaps that I have not found it so means nothing whatsoever. I may be but a Thomas among so many more of greater faith. We cannot say an angler is a bad angler who does badly on strange waters.

Who will dare to say that an angler is a bad angler because he does not make good catches from familiar streams? Familiarity with a stream may not breed contempt. But, I am sure, none of us live long enough to know so much of any water that we have mastered it.

I have fished a few streams many times but have mastered none of them. I hope I never will....

If we say we like to fish strange waters, this is no denial of a devotion to familiar streams. A new place is a new experience, and a new experience is to be desired....

If you have many years to your credit as an angler it will be easy for you to begin a story with, 'I remember the first time I fished...' You would be a disappointment to the whole art of angling if it were not so. A good angler is a good angler anywhere; even on strange waters.

A bad angler will not make a good catch no matter how often he explores a stretch of water. His handicap at the tenth visit is the same as when that stretch was strange water to him. If his hand has no cunning, his arm is not supple, his eye does not discern, his mind does not respond to signs and indications, then he had better leave strange waters alone. Likely enough he will do worse on them than even his worst on waters that have known him very likely far too long.

Strange waters key up your feelings of expectancy. There is not one place but has its new problem for you, no eddy that does not demand another and a different movement: each overhanging willow may become a landmark in your memory and earn its place in your stories of the stream.

Strange waters make many old things new. Your first day on them may be a blur of tangled memories as you end it. In time you find that at least one new thing has emerged, one new lesson has been well and truly learned; one new thrill has come your way, for which you are very grateful.

When you visit strange waters, go alone. You lose half the thrill if you take a local with you. Remember they are not strange to him. He may seem to help you. In fact, he only guides you to beaten paths and much fished water. There is no need for him unless it is to carry your lunch.

Play the game out with the stream! Go to it completely handicapped by all your ignorance. Then all you learn will be your very own.

Alexander and Angling
R. Sinclair Carr

The Dream

Sometimes, in the winter, which every dedicated fly-fisherman spends thinking about the next season, I have thought about my favourite sport and wondered what it is about it that gets under the skin of so many men; and why, once a man is really infected with the desire to catch trout and has caught his first two or three, he is powerless to give up and he may well begin to devote most of his wakeful hours to thinking about fishing. This is no joke. Many men are quite obsessed with fishing. Fly-fishing cannot be reckoned in terms of points or strokes, or handicaps. Every angler makes mistakes and is a master for a minute and a novice the next, and the mystery of a red-letter day leaves us all wondering how much better we might have done under different circumstances, or how we did so well when we apparently did exactly the same as on our off-days! It isn't the science of fishing. We can get that out of a book. It isn't the timing of a cast or the exact exertion in taking the line back and bringing it forward again. This skill can be imparted, taught, like the rudiments of any game in which a stick or a rod is used. It is, I am sure, the simple fascination of the dream, the day-dream, romance, uncertainty, if you like, or the mystery.

My own dreams run both ways. I dream of the burns and streams of my childhood and how I would fish them now, if I could, and if they could only contain those wonderful trout I used to see swinging in the shelter of great boulders and slabs of rock. The dream of yesterday is beautiful, for yesterday I had so much more time to wander by the burn or stand at the head of the loch seeing the fish rising out there on water that looked black because light was fading away. Yesterday I could have fished in a hundred places, when no petrol fumes drifted on the moorland road and the only sound was the crofter sharpening his scythe and the corncrake calling. How big the trout were and what dawns and sunrises we had! The bacon was salt and there were little bits of butter floating in the buttermilk I drank from a blue-ringed bowl, and my treasured possessions were a few hooks, a hand of gut, and a bit of line. Yesterday I was in danger of being drowned a dozen times and the family spread out in three or four directions, calling my name at nightfall, fearful that I had gone in over the ears and not just over my 'bootheads'. I long to fish those waters again, with my splitcane rod and flies I have made. Indeed, I fish them as I sit by the fire and catch those hard, plump fish that jerk and tug as I try to land them. I fish the water where the burn flows into the river, at evening when the midges roll beneath the willow tree's branches, and I come up home, to my grandfather's house, when the steading is in darkness and a pair of barn owls are sitting on the ridge. The house is asleep when I go in and I put my fine trout on the willow-patterned dish and go up to bed after I have had a bowl of water from the pump. Yesterday, alas, I didn't know what I know now about fishing, or about the world....

The dream of tomorrow is different. Experience tells me to temper the wildest dream with reason. There are no great fish in the little lake halfway up the mountain. There never have been and there never will be, and tomorrow if I must be content with going no farther than that I must also be content with the little fish that dwell there. Beyond this I may dream of the ripple and the sunrise, the clear water and the rings of rising fish all over the place, and what eager fish they are, taking the fly with such vigour that my heart jumps. Not every one is struck and not every one I play is landed, but I fish on and on in the warm sunshine with the cool breeze fanning my cheek and when I come home at evening

I leave the lake with the sun no longer touching it. By that time the ripple has been smoothed away and the last of the rise only serves to show that there are more fish to be caught, and there is a promise of another day. The dream is vast and unending. It takes me to a hundred lakes. I fish for char and catch them with the fly. I fish for a big trout and he will not go in my creel. I fish quietly in solitude and no one comes past me to cast a spinner where I caught a good one last season, or throws a shadow in a place I have been careful to approach with cunning. Fishing never measures up to the dream, of course, but each day builds the dream a little stronger. The fish of a pound-and-a-half caught in a place where

it wasn't expected makes it possible to imagine another capture of greater size, and that big fish comes as the other one came, and makes its battle and gives up. . . .

The dream sustains us in winter. It makes us leave a garden of weeds to go fishing. It makes us forget wife and children, our calling and our responsibilities. The world is, after all, a sort of a madhouse where everyone talks hard, drives hard, elbows, pushes and shoves and puts one over on his neighbor. Once, in the dim past, a man sat by a lake and caught himself a fish and all he had to worry about was that a wolf might be crawling up

on him or a member of a neighboring tribe watching him with a club ready in his hand. Everything in this man's world was in simple terms, however. He had few worries and he was an uncomplicated man, able to give his entire mind to the elementary thing that could bring a smile of simple delight to his face and make him utterly happy. Fly-fishing, although it doesn't stem from the caveman, is a simple pastime and it asks only that devotees give full attention to the principles in order to succeed. When a fly-fisherman is watching his line and his fly he can worry about nothing else, and the tension that normally grips him is relaxed for he is doing something new, something with imponderable

mystery about it and a business that cannot be solved with permutation or slide-rule. The dream comes after the relief of that first experience and the newcomer is drawn back again and again, like an infatuated lover. How many men have stood in the small hours of the morning, being eaten alive by midges while they tried to catch sea-trout? How many thousands of healthy, intelligent men have been caught up in the thing, like dallying schoolboys? The escape is a cure that must be repeated, but it is the dream, I think, that does most good, for the dream goes on and on, renewed day after day, month after month, season after season.

There is no weariness in the dream and the days are never cold. The rain never runs down one's collar, the line never sinks. Not every angler has the same experiences from which to build his dreams. Many a poor fellow builds success on failure and despair, or simply takes the story of an acquaintance and fires himself with enthusiasm to fish in a certain place. The hard facts are excluded from dreams, which is as it should be.

Trout from the Hills
Ian Niall

The Exhilaration of Danger

There are those who advance the theory that men
who engage in risk-action sports experience special
sensations..."mental and emotional elation during
risk-exercise can reach a euphoric state...sensations
that are at the far horizon of human elation."

"Danger as a Way of Joy"
William Furlong

The Sound of Thunder

One burn I used to fish flowed through a wood of
high trees down a steep rocky channel. Here it was
possible, at least for a small boy, to keep out of sight
by walking up the bed of the burn itself, stooping
low, jerking the worm up into little pools and
cascades above, and lifting the trout out down
stream on to the bank. This was very pretty work.
I remember once getting several trout quickly one
after the other in this place, and then they suddenly
stopped taking. One little favourite pool after
another produced nothing, and a fear of something
unknown came over me; the gloom and stillness of
the wood made me uneasy, everything about me
seemed to know something, to have a meaning,
which was hidden from me; and I felt as if my fishing
was out of place. At last I could resist the feeling of
apprehension no longer; I left the rod with the line
in a pool to fish for itself, and went up to the edge
of the wood to see what was happening in the open
world outside. There was a great storm coming up
full of awful menace, as thunderclouds often are. It
filled me with terror. I hurried back for my rod, left
the burn and the wood, and fled before the storm,
going slow to get breath now and then, and
continually urged to running again by the sound
of thunder behind me.

Fly Fishing
Viscount Grey of Fallodon

Trout in the Forests

The first work was the building of a raft. To the uninitiated it is often a puzzle how rafts are constructed by fishermen in the forests, and possibly there are not many sportsmen who have regarded an axe and an auger as parts of an outfit. The two things are essential to a forest expedition, and in going to fish an unknown sheet of water one might almost as well leave his rod behind him as these tools. There are ways of getting on without the auger, but a raft lashed together with withes is a dangerous craft. I have had such a one part with me in mid-lake, while I swam ashore with my rod in my hand, losing even the fish I had taken. In the present case I had both tools. The construction of the raft was very simple. Two pine trees supplied six logs, each about a foot in diameter, which were rolled into the water and floated side by side, a few inches apart. Across these, smaller timbers were laid, the axe shaping them down flat where wooden pegs were driven in auger holes through them into the heavy logs. It was but little over an hour's work to complete it, for the timber was at hand in good size and quantity. Then we covered the raft with balsam boughs, to stand or sit or lie down on, and a couple of long poles finished the furniture of the vessel on which we pushed out at the inlet of the lake. The day was so much more beautiful than the previous one that the lake appeared like a new place, and the trout were rising on the surface here and there in a way which indicated that the warm sunshine had brought out some small flies, invisible to the eye at a distance, but satisfactory as indicating that the fish were on the feed.

It was nearly ten o'clock when I began casting. But nothing rose to my flies till I had changed them twice or oftener, and had on three small gnats, a dun, a yellow and a black, and then came the first strike at the yellow, a half-pound fish soon killed. Another at the yellow, a somewhat larger fish, gave me some slight work, and a third took the yellow once more, and thereupon I changed: the dropper yellow, the tail fly yellow, and intermediate a small scarlet ibis. The first cast made with this new bank, as some men call the arrangement, cost me the scarlet fly. A large fish took the dropper, and at the same instant another struck the ibis. They headed on opposite directions, and the very stroke of the two parted the slender thread. I landed but one of that cast, and only once after that had two at the same time, and saved them both.

The sport continued good till about one o'clock, and then ceased. The breeze rippled the water, the flies were increasing in number in the warm sunshine, but feeding time was over and the fish went down. I have seen the same thing often on other waters.

The object of the expedition was accomplished. There were trout in the lake — they would rise to the fly. Over a dozen beautiful large fish, and nearly another dozen which ran below a half pound each, were fair evidence of the contents of this water.

An Exploring Expedition
W. C. Prime

Learning the Art

What is there to fly-fishing but the use of a rod, a line, a reel, and a fly to catch a trout? The rod is merely a means of getting the line to the fish. The reel, too, is a refinement. The cast is no more important than the line, even if a lump of rope would serve for neither. The essentials are the man, the fly, and the fish, but the secret lies in what the fish sees, not in what the man sees, or what he thinks the fish sees. The angler who goes to fish a lake must be ready for blank days while he is learning the art of fishing, but he must also be ready for nearly as many blank days while he is learning that no man knows it all, and no man can.

Trout from the Hills
Ian Niall

Birds

Waterside birds can make a large contribution to a day on a stream or a lake. I think we should be able to recognize most of them without difficulty and am always astonished because so many fishermen cannot. Heron, water ouzel, merganser, spotted sandpiper, osprey, kingfisher and many others are all part of going fishing and it is a great pity not to know them.

A good part of the pleasure of going fishing is in understanding these things, watching them and recording them in the mind, being able to name them and hold them for yourselves as valued things. Identifying them and knowing something about them gives you a special claim on your own world of the water's edge, and helps to make you a part of it instead of a mere intruder. This to me is a very important thing. It gives a sense of identification with the whole natural world which I think most of us are looking for. As nearly as I can find any one reason for why we go out to hunt and fish it is in this search for a sense of identification with the natural world. No one finds it more completely or more rewardingly than the fly fisherman. Yet in searching for it, we have no need to damage or reduce anything of this precious environment. If we understand our part, we can pass through that world with as little trace of ourselves and our passing as the Indian left when he passed before us.

A Talk to Fly Fishermen
Roderick Haig-Brown

A Huge Trout

The old beaver dam is still there, and over it the
water pours with soft noises into a deep and wide
pool. On one side of this dark bit of water is a great
rock. Its front is covered with thick mosses very rich
in color. Across it wanders a vine with little red
berries strung on it. Can you see the old beaver dam,
the pool, the big rock, the moss, the running vine
and the shining red berries? Yes? Very likely you
can; but, oh, you who have such eyes to see — you
cannot see the huge trout whose home that dark,
deep pool is, and which I have seen so many times
as he rose for the bug or grub that I tossed him.
And once as I lay on the edge of the pool, hidden in
the long grasses, I saw him at play, having a frolic
all by himself, and, oh, he made that space of
gloomy water iridescent as he flashed and flew
through it. Where is he? Do you really wish to know?
Well, I will be good and tell you. He is where
I found him.

Cones for the Campfire
W. H. H. Murray

Poaching

One must admit, rather sadly, that the old poacher has become a rarity. He belonged to the old estates and nearly all the fine estates have been broken up. Poachers there are, however, in the tradition. Now and again one is run to earth by a television interviewer and proves to be both garrulous and amusing, but the poachers of my youth were not garrulous. Country rascals, they may have been, under-privileged, the social reformer might call them, but resourceful men, and their sons and grandsons have stood more than once to defend the country that nurtured them. Many hard words were addressed to me for daring to produce a handbook on poaching, but I made no apology for it when it appeared, and I make none now, repeating my original preface which, I trust, will offend none but those whose liver is sadly out of order:

There is no better way of studying an art than by examining the technique of the masters, and the student will find in this modest work portraits of the men whose art has been recognized by authority; men who have devoted their lives to the subject, suffered severe penalties in the dogged pursuit of their calling — fines up to five pounds and many days in prison.

Poaching is said to be a dying art, but I do not believe this. No great art dies. Congenital poachers will father poachers. It is an old thing. Hunting is in the blood. So long as there is a warren to shelter a rabbit, a holly bush in which a bird roosts, and a hollow or a hill for a hare, there will be a man or a boy who will put his natural cunning to stalking the hare, hunting the wild things and out-witting both the quarry and the representative of authority.

If I have a decided sympathy for the ghost of the old poacher who still manages to touch the heart of many a just and upright magistrate when he comes to the dock, I have none for the gang, none for any save the individualist, the man whose skill and guile earned him his due reward and who was indeed often tolerated by the owner of land to an extent that infuriated his underlings. A word for the courage of the poachers in the days of pitched battles might be construed as indicating one's preference for anarchy, but I am not a man of violence. Anything can be taken by storm, a pheasant, or a citadel, and I would speak only of art and artifice. I can only add that these words are no apology for resurrecting a work that lays out a pattern of lawlessness. One doesn't make a poacher. He is born. Most readers, I think, will expect no apology and I trust that what I say will place none of them a pace beyond the line of recitude, nor take any of them away from a comfortable armchair and fire.

The New Poacher's Handbook
Ian Niall

We Could Not Hook Them

I remember that as on the first evening I came
joyously down from the cliff road on to the shingle-
bar, another angler was there wetting his line.
'These fish are devils to catch,' he cried out, 'got into
one the other day, I can't tell you how big he was,
perhaps five pounds; but he ran me out into the
middle of the lake, took off every inch of line, and
then snapped a length of strong Japanese gut as
if it were cotton.'
   I found it was exactly as he said. We could not get
them out. We could not even hook them. In the
evening, especially at sundown and just after, the
water was eloquent with trout. At the bottom end,
against and near the sand-bar, the shining water
was thickly patterned with the rings of their risings.
But we were quite out of it. We tried them with
nearly every fly in our books and dry-fly cases,
cast them right into the middle of the rings, and they
simply laughed at us with silent, mocking laughter,
and snatched down other flies within an inch of
ours. Plop! Plop! Up they came. But not at us.

The Roving Angler
Herbert E. Palmer

A Good Angler Never Feels Old

The first rush of a big trout is something worth
living for, and we are never sure of him until he is
in the basket. I have seen a two-pound fish landed
and then lost down a muskrat hole. If the trout leaps
at end of his first run, how enormous he appears!
I have been quite sure that a three-pounder weighed
at least five pounds. This is the right kind of
excitement. It rejuvenates an elderly man and takes
him back to the days of his boyhood; in fact a good
angler never feels old as long as he can cast his fly
to a rising trout.

Little Talks about Fly Fishing
Theodore Gordon

One of the Sure Paths to Health

When a man occupies his mind with this he must exclude the
mundane things. When he thinks about a trout turning, rising
gently to look at the fly and then making a rush to take it he
can think of nothing else. This must bring relief to his brain,
his tension. People smile at the idiosyncrasies of anglers, and
at their tall tales of the big fish that got away, but fishing,
I am convinced, is one of the sure paths to physical and mental
health. A fisherman may have ulcers but fishing does his
ulcers good. I doubt whether any other sport could do them
quite so much good, for as the trout rises and the line begins
to cut the water as it runs, he would be a poor man who was
not transported, uplifted and removed entirely from the dreary
background of his everyday thoughts and worries.

Trout from the Hills
Ian Niall

The Art of Trout Fishing

Angling, or the art of capturing fish with rod and hook, appears perfectly simple to those unacquainted with the subject; and unlimited patience is not unfrequently looked upon as the only qualification necessary for success. That this is an error is shown by experience; there being numbers of the very best anglers who are by no means celebrated as possessing this virtue, while number of the most patient followers of Izaak Walton are very far from having rivalled his success. Few amusements require more skill, or afford more room for the exercise of ingenuity; and practice will render a greater proportion of individuals successful shots than successful anglers.

There can be no better proof of the difficulty of excelling in this art than the fact that, out of the thousands who practice it, very few become proficient; and since the pleasure of a pastime depends to a great extent upon the field it affords

for the exercise of skill, angling is well worthy of the attention of sportsmen.

One qualification which he who wishes to become an angler must not only possess, but must exert to the utmost, is observation. He may have all the other qualifications necessary — neatness of hand, quickness of eye, energy, and perseverance — but to become acquainted with the habits of the fish, the places to which they resort in search of particular kinds of food, and the influence of the weather upon them requires keen observation and great experience. With observation, most people may become anglers; without it no one will ever achieve great success.

To the lover of nature no sport affords so much pleasure. The grandest and most picturesque scenes in nature are to be found on the banks of rivers and lakes. The angler, therefore, enjoys the finest scenery the country offers, and the season of the year most

suitable to his pastime is that which nature is clothed in her most brilliant colors.

Of all the inhabitants of the fresh water, no fish is looked upon with such favour by the angler, and none affords him such varied and continuous sport as the common fresh-water trout. This is owing to its being the most difficult to capture of all the finny tribe, not excepting the salmon itself, to the sport it affords when hooked — the trout being stronger than any fish of its size — to its fine edible qualities, and to the fact that it rises to the artificial fly.

On a holiday, the banks of any stream in the neighborhood of a large town are thickly studded with anglers, a few of whom meet with good sport, but the greater number, having demolished their sandwiches, return with their baskets lighter than when they left home. Happily, however, and it is certainly a strong argument in favour of the attractions of angling, they are not a whit discouraged; but, on the contrary, eager to return at first opportunity, and have always a good excuse for their want of success.

We have never yet met a bad angler that had not a good excuse; sometimes it is clear water, sometimes a bright day, sometimes thunder in the air; but the great excuse, which is equally applicable to all states of weather and water, is that, somehow or other, the trout would not take.

Anglers there are who never yet met the trout in taking humor, and never will, unless they alter their mode of fishing. They have also an extraordinary knack of raising, hooking, and playing, but losing large trout. The trout once escaped, there is ample scope for the imagination to conjecture its probable size.

The Practical Angler
W. C. Stewart

The Inward Qualities of a Skillful Angler

Now for the inward qualities of the minde, albeit some Writers
reduce them into twelve heads, which indeed whosoever
injoyeth cannot chuse but be very compleat in much perfection,
yet I must draw them into many more Branches.

The First, and most especiall whereof, is, that a skilfull Angler
ought to bee a generall Scholler, and seene in all the Liberall
Sciences, as a Gramarian, to know how either to Write or
Discourse of his Art in true and fitting termes, either without
affectation or rudeness. Hee should have sweetnes of speech to
perswade and intice other to delight in an Exercise so much
Laudable. Hee should have strength of arguments to defend
and maintane his profession, against Envy or slaunder.

Hee should have knowledge in the Sunne, Moone, and
Starres, that by their Aspects hee may guesse the
seasonablenesse, or unseasonablenesse of the weather, the
breeding of stormes, and from what coasts the Windes are ever
delivered....

Hee should bee a good knower of Countries, and well used to high wayes, that by taking the readiest pathes to every Lake, Brooke, or River, his journies may be more certaine, and lesse wearisome. Hee should have knowledge in proportions of all sorts, whether Circular, Square, or, Diametricall, that when hee shall be questioned of his diurnall progresses, hee may give a Geographicall description of the Angles and Channels of Rivers, how they fall from their heads, and what compasses they fetch in their severall windings.

Hee must also have the perfect Art of numbring, that in the soundings of Lakes or Rivers, hee may know how many foot or inches each severally contayneth, and by adding, subtracting, or multiplying the same, hee may yeeld the reason of every Rivers swift or slow Current....

Then hee must be full of love, both to his pleasure and to his Neighbor; To his pleasure which otherwise would be irkesome and tedious, and to his neighbor that he neither give offence in any particular, nor be guilty of any general distruction.

Then he must be exceeding patient, and neither vexe or excruciate himselfe with losses or mischances, as in losing the prey when it is almost in the hand, or by breaking his Tooles by ignorance or negligence, but with a pleased sufferance amend his errors, and thinke mischances instructions to better carefullnesse.

He must then be full of humble thoughts, not disdayning when occasion commands to kneele, lye downe, or wet his feet or fingers, as oft as there is any advantage given thereby, unto the gaining the end of his labour.

Then he must be strong and valiant, neither to be amazed with stormes, nor affrighted with thunder, but to hold them according to their naturall causes, and the pleasure of the Highest: neither must he, like the Foxe, which preyeth upon Lambes, imploy all his labour against a smaller frie, but like the Lyon that feazeth Elephants, thinke the greatest Fish which swimmeth, a reward lille enough for the paines which he endureith....

Then must he be liberall, and not working onely for his owne belly, as if it could never be satisfied; but he must with much cheerfulnesse bestow the fruites of his skill amongst his honest neighbours, who being partners of his game, will doubly renown his tryumph, and that is ever pleasing reward to vertue.

Then he musst be prudent, that apprehending the Reasons why the Fish will note bite, and all other casuall impediments which hinder his sport, and knowing the Remedies for them same, hee may direct his Labours to be without trouble fommesse: Then he must have a moderate contention of the mind, to be satisfied with indifferent things, and not out of an avaricious greedinesse thinke every thing too little, be it never so abundant.

Then must he be of a thankeful nature, praising the Author of all goodnesse, and shewing a large gratefulnesse for the least satisfaction.

Then must he bee of a perfect memory, quicke, and prompt to call into his mind all the needful things which are any way in his Exercise to be imployed, lest by omission or by forgetfulnesse of any, he frustrate his hopes, and make his Labour effectlesse.

Lastly, he must be of a strong constitution of body, able to endure much fasting, and not of a gnawing stromacke, observing houres, in which if it be unsatisfied, it troubleth both the mind and body, and loseth that delight which maketh the pastime onely pleasing.

Country Contentment
Gervase Markham

One of the greatest charms in fly fishing is that you never can learn it all even in the longest life. I have been at it for about forty years and I am always learning something new. Every new stream will teach you something new if you keep your eyes open.

A Book on Angling
Francis Francis

Fly fishing
is a fair contest
between the fish
and the man.
Success depends solely
on the caprice
of the fish,
your own skill
and perseverance.
That is much.

Fishing & Shooting
Sidney Buxton

Bibliography

Brennand, George   *Halcyon*. London: A. & C.
   Black, 1947

Buxton, Sidney   *Fishing And Shooting*. London:
   John Murray, 1902

Carr, R. Sinclair   *Alexander And Angling*. London: Chatto
   and Windus, 1936

Ciccimara, Richard   *The Cowichan*. Portland, Oregon: *The Creel*,
   Vol. 4, No. 1; The Bulletin of the Flyfisher's Club of Oregon

Farson, Negley   *Going Fishing*. London: 1949

Fedden, Romilly   *Golden Days*. London: A. & C. Black, 1949

Francis, Francis   *A Book On Angling*. London: Longmans, Green & Co., 1885

Gordon, Theodore   *Little Talks About Fly Fishing* from *The
   Complete Fly Fisherman* by John McDonald. New York: Charles
   Scribner's Sons, 1947

Grey, Viscount   *Fly Fishing*. London: J. M. Dent & Sons Ltd., 1930

Haig-Brown, Roderick   *A River Never Sleeps*. New York: Wm. Morrow
   & Company, 1946; *Fisherman's Fall*. New York: Wm. Morrow & Company,
   1964

Hillaby, John   *Within The Streams*. London: Harvey & Blythe, 1949

Hills, John W.   *River Keeper*. London: Geoffrey Bles, 1947

Kipling, Rudyard   *American Notes*. Philadelphia: Henry Altemus, 1899

Lampman, Ben Hur   *Opening Day* from *A Leaf From French Eddy*.
   Portland, Oregon: Touchstone Press, 1965; *A Farewell To 'Tige'*,
   and *Where Would You Go?* Portland Oregonian, 1932

Lockhart, Sir Robert Bruce   *My Rod, My Comfort*. London: Putnam & Co., 1959

Markham, Gervase   *Country Contentment*. London: 1683

Murray, W. H. H.   *Cones For The Campfire*. Boston, 1891

Niall, Ian   *Trout From The Hills*. London: Wm. Heinemann, Ltd. 1961

Palmer, Herbert E.   *The Roving Angler*. London: 1947

Perry, Bliss   *Pools & Ripples*. Boston: Little, Brown & Co., 1927

Peterson, Edwin L.   *No Life So Happy*. New York: Dodd, Mead & Co., 1940

Prime, William C.   *I Go A Fishing*. New York: 1876

Ruskin, John   *Modern Painters*, Sec. V, Vol. 11. London: 1846

Stewart, W. C.   *Practical Angler*. London: 1919

A Note on Photography

Should the reader be interested in combining the pleasures of
fly fishing and photography, he will find an abundance of
technical information available on cameras, lenses, films and
accessories in any reputable camera store. To be practical about
it, of course, one must keep his equipment simple. Here are
some hints and suggestions:

Choose a 35mm camera with a built-in light meter and
interchangeable lenses.

For black and white photographs use Plus-X (fine grain) film
for normal or bright days, and Tri-X (faster, coarser grain) for
dark overcast days, early morning or late evening shooting.

For color photographs use Kodachrome, Ektachrome-X, or
High Speed Ektachrome which is useful for fast action shots or
greater depth of focus. A skylight filter will cut through the
haze for color photography and protect your lens.

Desirable lenses are the basic 50mm lens which comes with
the camera, a close-up lens, a wide-angle lens and a telephoto
lens—possibly one of the new zoom lenses.

The use of filters will give you more dramatic black and white
photographs. The orange filter, which I used for most of the
black and white photographs in this book, creates moderate
contrasts while the red filter gives much stronger contrasts.

A small brush to dust the lens is essential. Also, lens paper
and cleaning fluid—*a lens must always be immaculate*. Another
useful item is a tiny screwdriver to tighten the minute screws
which can work loose on a lens or the camera case.